Intersections:
Where Faith and Life Meet

A Cumberland Presbyterian Adult Resource
Volume 10, Love

Discipleship Ministry Team
Ministry Council
Cumberland Presbyterian Church

8207 Traditional Place
Cordova, Tennessee 38016

© 2015 Discipleship Ministry Team

All Rights Reserved. No part of this book may be reproduced or transmitted in any form or by any means, electronic or mechanical, including photocopying, recording, or by any information storage or retrieval system, without permission in writing from the publisher. For information contact Discipleship Ministry Team, Cumberland Presbyterian Center, 8207 Traditional Place, Cordova, Tennessee, 38016-7414.

First Edition 2015

Published by The Discipleship Ministry Team
General Assembly Ministry Council of the Cumberland Presbyterian Church
Cordova, Tennessee

ISBN-13: 978-0692566244
ISBN-10: 0692566244

We want to hear from you.
Please send your comments about this curriculum to
the Discipleship Ministry Team at chm@cumberland.org.

OUR UNITED OUTREACH
Made Possible In Part By Your Tithe To Our United Outreach

Table of Contents

Lesson 1 Love as Reconciliation 4

Lesson 2 Love as Covenant 14

Lesson 3 Love Is Costly 24

Lesson 4 Love Isn't Always Pretty 33

Lesson 5 Love that Changes Everything 43

Lesson 6 Love Is a Verb 52

Lesson 7 Love as the Way 61

Lesson 8 Love Is from God 70

Unless otherwise specified, all scripture text is from the New Revised Standard Version Bible, copyright 1989, Division of Christian Education of the National Council of the Churches of Christ in the United States of America. Used by permission. All rights reserved.

Editor: Cindy Martin
Designer: Joanna Wilkinson
Proofreader: Mark Taylor

To order, call 901-276-4572, x 252 or e-mail resources@cumberland.org.

Love as Reconciliation

Scripture for lesson:
Genesis 29:15-20; 37:1-4, 12-24; 45:4-5; 50:15-21

Written by Whitney Brown

We hear the word *love* a lot these days. We use it in many different ways. "I love my new phone"; "I love those earrings"; "I love Saturdays." We certainly don't mean we care as much about these things as we do our family and friends, but we use the word *love* so much that it has lost some of its meaning. Yet there are other times when we express or experience love through actions, often without use of the word. In those times, we experience love in a deep and meaningful way.

Prep for the Journey

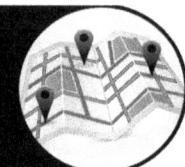

Although he was a forefather of Israel, Jacob had quite a rocky start in developing good character. Jacob was the second son of Isaac and the grandson of Abraham. You may recall that Jacob had a twin brother, Esau, from whom he managed to finagle the birthright and blessings reserved for the firstborn.

After deceiving his ailing father and stealing the blessing that had been meant for Esau, Isaac fled from his home, afraid his brother would kill him. As he was his mother's favorite child, she sent him to her brother, who lived near Haran, where she thought he would be safe. I can imagine that both Jacob and his mother anticipated that he would return once Esau had had the chance to "cool off."

As Jacob approached Haran, he saw shepherds gathered with their flocks. Because the stone that covered the well was very large, all of the shepherds would gather at the same time in order to move it and give their sheep a drink. When Jacob inquired about his uncle, Laban, he was told that the approaching shepherdess was his cousin, the daughter of Laban.

Rachel, Laban's daughter, was very lovely, and Jacob was taken with her upon their first meeting. In typical "stud" fashion, Jacob

---

> How often do you use the word *love*? What do you mean when you say it? What other words might be more appropriate at times?

> How do you feel about someone with Jacob's background having been instrumental in the history of God's people?

moved the rock covering the well by himself and watered Rachel's flock. Then he kissed Rachel.

A kiss so quickly might seem a bit fast for us, but Jacob had endured a long, lonely, and dangerous journey. To find that he had finally reached his destination caused him great joy. Upon learning of Jacob's identity, Rachel ran to find her father. We can only guess as to why she didn't take Jacob with her! Laban came quickly, and after some "getting to know you" questions, he accepted that Jacob was indeed his nephew.

When I was a child, family members who lived in another state would periodically just appear at our door. Invariably, they would come when my mother was very busy canning and freezing garden produce. We never knew when they were coming nor how long they would stay. Sometimes they would help with the household chores, but they still created more work for our family because of the extra food preparation and interruption of routine chores.

Laban found himself in somewhat the same situation as my family. After Jacob had been there for a month, Laban began to realize that this was likely going to be an extended visit. Apparently Jacob had been lending a hand with the work, and Laban felt that he needed to be compensated.

Read Genesis 29:15-20.

Then Laban said to Jacob, "Because you are my kinsman, should you therefore serve me for nothing? Tell me, what shall your wages be?" ¹⁶Now Laban had two daughters; the name of the elder was Leah, and the name of the younger was Rachel. ¹⁷Leah's eyes were lovely, and Rachel was graceful and beautiful. ¹⁸Jacob loved Rachel; so he said, "I will serve you seven years for your younger daughter Rachel." ¹⁹Laban said, "It is better that I give her to you than that I should give her to any other man; stay with me." ²⁰So Jacob served seven years for Rachel, and they seemed to him but a few days because of the love he had for her.

Jacob worked for Laban for seven years with the promise of marriage to Rachel as his wages. At the end of the seven years, Laban instead gave his older daughter, Leah, to Jacob, claiming that it was traditional for the older daughter to marry before the younger one could. Although Laban agreed to let Jacob marry Rachel sooner, Jacob had to work another seven years for her.

On the Road

Jacob labored for fourteen years in order to marry the one he loved. During this time, Jacob endured more tricks from Laban, who

---

Have you ever met or learned about a long lost relative? How did you feel? How did you establish connections?

How do you react if someone unexpectedly comes to visit, even if only for a couple of hours?

When have you done something because you loved the person? How did your love for the person affect the attitude with which you approached the task?

> When have you seen favoritism create problems in families? If you have experienced favoritism, how did you feel? react? What were the reactions of others who were involved?

seemed intent on cheating Jacob at every opportunity. While all of this was going on, things on the "home front" were not peaceful either.

Just imagine two sisters married to the same man. Leah knew that Jacob loved Rachel, not her. So she tried to win his love by bearing children, which her sister seemed unable to do. Finally, Rachel conceived and bore Joseph a son. However, trouble again reared its head. The trouble centered on Joseph, Rachel's first son and Jacob's favorite child.

Read Genesis 37:1-4.

Jacob settled in the land where his father had lived as an alien, the land of Canaan. ²This is the story of the family of Jacob. Joseph, being seventeen years old, was shepherding the flock with his brothers; he was a helper to the sons of Bilhah and Zilpah, his father's wives; and Joseph brought a bad report of them to their father. ³Now Israel loved Joseph more than any other of his children, because he was the son of his old age; and he had made him a long robe with sleeves. ⁴But when his brothers saw that their father loved him more than all his brothers, they hated him, and could not speak peaceably to him.

Joseph was one of only two sons Rachel bore to Jacob. Jacob had ten other sons by his three other wives. Rachel died when giving birth to her second son, Benjamin. Because Joseph was the son of his beloved Rachel, Jacob favored him, which was obvious to everyone, including Joseph's brothers. Joseph made matters worse by reveling in the favoritism, "lording it over them," so to speak.

Jacob gave Joseph a special robe. Some versions of the scripture call it a robe of many colors; other versions refer to it as a robe with sleeves. Neither of these robes would have been conducive to the work of a shepherd. In other words, while his half-brothers were out working, Joseph was living the life of the spoiled, rich kid.

Joseph was not a very likable person. He was a tattle tale, and he had the audacity to tell about a dream in which all of his family bowed down to him.

> When have you encountered someone whom you loved to hate? How did you learn to deal with this person? What would it take for you to love this person?

Read Genesis 37:12-24.

Now his brothers went to pasture their father's flock near Shechem. ¹³And Israel said to Joseph, "Are not your brothers pasturing the flock at Shechem? Come, I will send you to them." He answered, "Here I am." ¹⁴So he said to him, "Go now, see if it is well with your brothers and with the flock; and bring word back to me." So he sent him from the valley of Hebron. He came to Shechem, ¹⁵and a man found him wandering in the fields; the man asked him, "What are you seeking?" ¹⁶"I am seeking my brothers," he said; "tell me, please, where they are pasturing the flock." ¹⁷The man said, "They have gone away, for I heard them say, 'Let us go to Dothan.'" So Joseph went after his brothers, and found them at Dothan. ¹⁸They saw him from a distance, and before he came near to them, they conspired to kill him. ¹⁹They said to one another, "Here

Joseph demonstrated to his family, reflects the purity of what we pray when we say, "Your Kingdom come, your will be done, on Earth as it is in Heaven."

In the Rear View

Jacob and Joseph are most often remembered as patriarchs, great leaders in the formation of our faith. Jacob inherited God's promises through his father, Isaac, even though he stole that blessing from his brother. Joseph, the dreamer, overcame deception, slavery, lies, and imprisonment to save his family and the people of Egypt from the famine.

In order to understand the great love to which God calls us, we must better understand the brokenness among and within the people to whom that love is sent. Understanding the context and fuller story of the ancestors of our faith, their brokenness and misdeeds, does not discredit the wonders God has done through them. It makes these stories, and ours, whole.

> Who has been instrumental in the formation of your faith?

Travel Log

Day 1:

Look up the words *reconciliation*, *redemption*, and *love*. What do you discover? How do these words give hope to your life? Make some notes about where you need to offer and receive reconciliation, redemption, and love.

Day 2:

As we saw in this dysfunctional family, love can be found in unlikely places. Reflect on one of those unlikely places in your own history. Journal about your experience.

Day 3:
   Being the favorite did not work out so well for these biblical characters. When has showing favor or being the favorite caused trouble for you? Write down any instances of favoritism of which you have been guilty. Offer a prayer of forgiveness, and consider writing a letter of apology to the persons whom you slighted.

Day 4:
   In order to bring reconciliation, we must acknowledge the broken systems and relationships at work in our lives and communities. List the specific needs in your community/family/life to which you are most drawn. Choose one of those needs, and share your passion for reconciling the brokenness with someone else.

Day 5:

Think of a time when you have served others. How did the people you served teach you about love? Journal about one or more of these experiences.

Day 6:

How does recognizing the deep areas of brokenness throughout the lineage of our faith story affect your faith or understanding of scripture? Record your responses here.

Day 7:

We know that Joseph was not perfect, so reconciling with his family no doubt meant dealing with a host of emotions. What might you have been thinking and feeling if you had been in Joseph's place when his brothers came for food? How do you balance those thoughts and emotions in a way that allows for reconciliation and peace to come to such a damaged relationship? Where does that need to happen in your own life?

Create a list of action steps for how you will work for reconciliation. Then establish a time line for following through with the steps.

Love as Covenant

Scripture for lesson:
1 Samuel 3:19-21; 8:19-22; 15:35; 16:1, 11-12, 19, 21-22; 18:1, 3-4; 19:1-7; 20:1-4, 16-17, 41-42

Written by Whitney Brown

Promises, promises. We make many promises to those we love. Marriages begin with vows. Ministers commit to believe and uphold the promises they make when they are ordained. Our lives are covered in promises!

Some promises are given casually; while the likely intent is to keep them, they are not binding. Other promises are considered to be binding; we call those types of promises covenants. God makes covenants. Humans make covenants. Some covenants have conditions, and others will be upheld regardless of the other party's faithfulness.

The Cumberland Presbyterian Church is said to have a theology sewn together with "a covenant of grace." As believers in this covenant, we understand that it is God's work, God's reconciling love, and the new covenant made through Jesus Christ that give us hope and lead us to be agents of change in a broken world.

Prep for the Journey

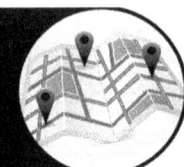

First Samuel continues the story of God's people. It follows the events of a priest named Samuel who also served as a prophet and judge over Israel. Some people will remember Samuel from the story of his mother dedicating him to God in response to God having answered her prayers for a child. Samuel grew up at Shiloh, a place of worship, under the tutelage of Eli the priest.

God spoke to Samuel one night when he was just a boy, calling to him shortly after he had gone to bed. Samuel thought Eli had called him, but Eli finally realized that God had been speaking to the child. God told Samuel what was going to happen to Eli's sons, who had been blaspheming God. Eli knew of his sons' actions, but had not tried to stop them. Consequently, God would punish his family forever.

What covenants have you made? What does "a covenant of grace" mean to you?

When have you been responsible for sharing bad news with someone? How did you approach this task?

Read 1 Samuel 3:19-21.

As Samuel grew up, the LORD was with him and let none of his words fall to the ground. ²⁰And all Israel from Dan to Beer-sheba knew that Samuel was a trustworthy prophet of the LORD. ²¹The LORD continued to appear at Shiloh, for the LORD revealed himself to Samuel at Shiloh by the word of the LORD.

As judge over Israel, Samuel served as God's spokesperson to them. He also served as a military deliverer, going into battle with the military leaders or seeking God's will before they entered into combat. In other words, Samuel and God lead the people as a kind of team.

When the people decided that they needed a king, Samuel tried to talk them out of it. Their enemies, with armies led by kings, were growing stronger. The tribes of Israel were scattered throughout the land of Canaan. Not only were they not one nation, they even fought among themselves. Each tribe had leaders and they had not all remained faithful to God, so they didn't necessarily even have faith as a unifying element. Despite Samuel's warning about what life under the leadership of a king would be like, the people continued to call for a new leader.

Read 1 Samuel 8:19-22.

But the people refused to listen to the voice of Samuel; they said, "No! but we are determined to have a king over us, ²⁰so that we also may be like other nations, and that our king may govern us and go out before us and fight our battles." ²¹When Samuel had heard all the words of the people, he repeated them in the ears of the LORD. ²²The LORD said to Samuel, "Listen to their voice and set a king over them." Samuel then said to the people of Israel, "Each of you return home."

God instructed Samuel to anoint Saul as king over Israel. All was well for a while as Saul led the people in defeat of their enemies, but then Saul sinned against God and his heart turned away from serving God. Although he would continue to reign until his death, Saul's unfaithfulness meant that his family would not continue to rule in Israel.

Read 1 Samuel 15:35.

Samuel did not see Saul again until the day of his death, but Samuel grieved over Saul. And the LORD was sorry that he had made Saul king over Israel.

On the Road

While Samuel mourned Saul, God had already chosen Saul's successor. However, Samuel wasn't so sure about God's plan to anoint someone else to be king.

When have you insisted on having something even when others warned you that it was not in your best interest? What happened after you got it? How did you deal with any repercussions?

What parallels do you see between the situation with Saul and world rulers over the past fifty years? Samuel called Saul out for his unfaithfulness. Who calls out today's leaders when they are not faithful?

When have you questioned God's plan? What happened?

> Why have God's choices of leaders sometimes surprised you? When have you witnessed an unlikely person become a strong leader?

Read 1 Samuel 16:1, 11-12.

The LORD said to Samuel, "How long will you grieve over Saul? I have rejected him from being king over Israel. Fill your horn with oil and set out; I will send you to Jesse the Bethlehemite, for I have provided for myself a king among his sons."

...

¹¹Samuel said to Jesse, "Are all your sons here?" And he said, "There remains yet the youngest, but he is keeping the sheep." And Samuel said to Jesse, "Send and bring him; for we will not sit down until he comes here." ¹²He sent and brought him in. Now he was ruddy, and had beautiful eyes, and was handsome. The Lord said, "Rise and anoint him; for this is the one."

God had chosen a boy to be the next king of Israel! In fact, his father had to send for him because he was tending the sheep. He was not thought old enough to participate in the sacrifice to which Samuel had invited his father and brothers.

When God's spirit departed from Saul, he began to be tormented by an evil spirit. Someone suggested that he might be helped during those times of rage by having someone play soothing music. A member of the king's court knew of David's musical ability and recommended him to Saul.

Read 1 Samuel 16:19, 21-22.

So Saul sent messengers to Jesse, and said, "Send me your son David who is with the sheep."... ²¹And David came to Saul, and entered his service. Saul loved him greatly, and he became his armor-bearer. ²²Saul sent to Jesse, saying, "Let David remain in my service, for he has found favor in my sight."

Jonathan was Saul's son. In terms of monarchies, Jonathan should have been next in line to ascend the throne of Israel. Jonathan was a successful military leader and had all the makings of a king who would bring victory and success to the kingdom.

Read 1 Samuel 18:1, 3-4.

When David had finished speaking to Saul, the soul of Jonathan was bound to the soul of David, and Jonathan loved him as his own soul. ...³Then Jonathan made a covenant with David, because he loved him as his own soul. ⁴Jonathan stripped himself of the robe that he was wearing, and gave it to David, and his armor, and even his sword and his bow and his belt.

There are some people with whom we feel an almost instantaneous connection upon meeting them. We don't know what the specific connection was between David and Jonathan, but it must have been immediate. Their relationship continues to be held up as one of true friendship and love.

It was common for people of that time to exchange clothing as a way to seal a new friendship. We don't know at what point it became known or obvious to Jonathan that David would be the next king of

> What covenants, promises, or commitments have you made? What covenants and commitments does your church hold?

Israel rather than himself. However, he had already formed a strong friendship with David, which was not affected by the news. In fact, Jonathan pledged loyalty to David rather than desiring the throne for himself and his father's household.

Scenic Route

After David defeated Goliath, he became known throughout the kingdom. He was handsome, brave, and likable, which made him popular with the people. However, it is unlikely that Saul appointed David over the army as this time; David would still have been a youth. David's popularity, though, did become an issue for Saul, causing him to envy David, whom he had appointed as his armor bearer and made a permanent resident of the palace. Saul became angry, jealous, and fearful as he sensed that God's favor had left him and was with David. A prisoner to his fear, Saul made multiple attempts on David's life.

Read 1 Samuel 19:1-7.

Saul spoke with his son Jonathan and with all his servants about killing David. But Saul's son Jonathan took great delight in David. ²Jonathan told David, "My father Saul is trying to kill you; therefore be on guard tomorrow morning; stay in a secret place and hide yourself. ³I will go out and stand beside my father in the field where you are, and I will speak to my father about you; if I learn anything I will tell you." ⁴Jonathan spoke well of David to his father Saul, saying to him, "The king should not sin against his servant David, because he has not sinned against you, and because his deeds have been of good service to you; ⁵for he took his life in his hand when he attacked the Philistine, and the Lord brought about a great victory for all Israel. You saw it, and rejoiced; why then will you sin against an innocent person by killing David without cause?" ⁶Saul heeded the voice of Jonathan; Saul swore, "As the Lord lives, he shall not be put to death." ⁷So Jonathan called David and related all these things to him. Jonathan then brought David to Saul, and he was in his presence as before.

Jonathan risked opposing his own father to save David's life. While he was successful in this first attempt, the peace would not last. As David continued to gain popularity, Saul again sought to kill him. With the help of Michal (Saul's daughter and one of David's wives) and Samuel, David escaped.

Read 1 Samuel 20:1-4.

David fled from Naioth in Ramah. He came before Jonathan and said, "What have I done? What is my guilt? And what is my sin against your father that he is trying to take my life?" ²He said to him, "Far from

---

When have you experienced a love that would lead you to put everything you own, everything rightfully yours, on the line and freely give it to another person?

Of what are you a prisoner? What would free you?

How can the faith community help to resolve conflict? What is our responsibility to do so?

it! You shall not die. My father does nothing either great or small without disclosing it to me; and why should my father hide this from me? Never!" ³But David also swore, "Your father knows well that you like me; and he thinks, 'Do not let Jonathan know this, or he will be grieved.' But truly, as the Lord lives and as you yourself live, there is but a step between me and death." ⁴Then Jonathan said to David, "Whatever you say, I will do for you."

David and Jonathan devised a plan to determine whether or not David would be safe in Saul's presence. Jonathan knew that going against his father could have meant losing the kingdom at best and his own death at worst, but he agreed anyway.

Read 1 Samuel 20:16-17.

Thus Jonathan made a covenant with the house of David, saying, "May the Lord seek out the enemies of David." ¹⁷Jonathan made David swear again by his love for him; for he loved him as he loved his own life.

> It is apparent that Saul was suffering from a mental disease. Many people in our society struggle with mental issues and diseases. How can the faith community reach out to these people, helping them to feel welcomed and included rather than ostracized?

As Jonathan put the plan into action, he learned that Saul was intently focused on killing David. When Jonathan tried to lie for David, Saul became enraged and threw a spear at Jonathan. The next day Jonathan went to the field where David was hiding. Jonathan sent the agreed-upon signal that it was no longer safe for David at the palace or anywhere near Saul.

Read 1 Samuel 20:41-42.

As soon as the boy had gone, David rose from beside the stone heap and prostrated himself with his face to the ground. He bowed three times, and they kissed each other, and wept with each other; David wept the more. ⁴²Then Jonathan said to David, "Go in peace, since both of us have sworn in the name of the Lord, saying, 'The Lord shall be between me and you, and between my descendants and your descendants, forever.'" He got up and left; and Jonathan went into the city.

> When have you had to say good bye to a close friend or relative, knowing you might not see that person again? How did you feel?
>
> What would allow you to grieve for someone who had tried to kill you?

As far as we know, this is the last time David and Jonathan saw each other. David fled, and Saul continued to track him in hopes of killing him. The book of First Samuel concludes with Saul's death, and Second Samuel begins with a messenger telling David of the death of both Saul and Jonathan. David grieved deeply at the loss of both men.

Workers Ahead

The beautiful thing about biblical covenants (especially those made by God) is that rarely do the two parties enter into the covenant on equal ground. They are, therefore, covenants of grace; parties who were once unequal become bound to one another in the covenantal relationship. Again, we see an image of the reconciling work of God with creation. In the example of David and Jonathan, Jonathan was the next rightful king in earthly terms. He had the bloodline, the training, the treasures of royalty, but David was anointed. He had God's blessing. In most stories, this plot would have set the stage for a violent feud between David and Jonathan. Instead, we see a covenant of grace as two souls bound together pledged to love and protect one another when violence surrounded them.

The Cumberland Presbyterian *Confession of Faith* states the following concerning covenantal relationships: "God acts to restore sinful persons to a covenant relationship, the nature of which is that of a family. It is established through God's initiative and the human response of faith. God's covenant is a relationship of grace. It appears in various forms and manifestations in the scriptures but always as one of grace. The new covenant in Jesus Christ is its ultimate and supreme expression" (3.02-3.03).

In the Rear View

While covenants are often seen as promises made between two people, we know of many examples where covenants are made as a community. In the *Confession of Faith*, the church is seen as the covenant community. We are people living under the new covenant, the receivers of the reconciliation brought by Jesus. We carry with us, and profess the hope of, that new covenant. We are called to extend that same hope to the world. Just as God made a covenant to love us unconditionally, so we share and extend the good news of that covenant in our homes and communities.

> Who or what are the would-be rivals to your faith community? What would it mean to extend a covenant of grace to those people/places? How could you do so?

> How are you sharing the hope and love of new covenant with the world?

Travel Log

Day 1:

Reflect about the covenant of grace and what it means to you. How will living in a covenant of grace affect your life this week? Journal your thoughts in this space.

Day 2:

Saul was Israel's first king. Samuel warned the people that a monarchy would bring unrest, but they continued to demand a king. Reflect about a time when you received something you really wanted, only to find out later that it was not all you had hoped. Or, think of a time when things did not go according to plan, but ended up better than you had expected.

Day 3:

David was a shepherd boy from a small town when he was called to the palace. He must have felt overwhelmed by all that was happening to and around him. Yet, God's spirit was with David.

When have you felt overwhelmed? How did you cope with those feelings? How did you sense God's presence during those times?

Day 4:

Jonathan loved David more than he loved himself. List the ways people in your life have shown you selfless love. How and when have you have done the same to others?

Day 5:

Fear and envy caused much of Saul's anger. He feared that God had left him. He feared that he would lose everything to David. He envied David's popularity and abilities. The fear and envy drove him crazy.

As Christians, we are called to live and give freely through the love God shows us. Journal about the fears that keep you from being fully free. Consider how love can free you from those fears.

Day 6:

Promises can be, and often are, broken. It doesn't matter on which side of the broken promise you find yourself, it is painful. Who do you need to forgive for breaking a promise to you? From whom do you need to seek forgiveness due to a broken promise? Make note of those names here. Take time today to contact those people from whom you need to seek forgiveness.

Day 7:
    David and Jonathan had the kind of friendship that not all people are fortunate enough to experience. List the names of your friends. Write beside each name at least one thing that you appreciate about the friendship. Contact that person and share your appreciation for your friendship.

Love Is Costly

Scripture for lesson:
Matthew 10:26-38; Luke 6:27-35;
John 3:16-17; 13:1-5, 34-35

Written by Whitney Brown

How would you define love? When have you experienced costly love?

My high school economics teacher began our first class by saying, "Nothing in life is free…except maybe love. Love is free." It's true that love is something we can freely give and receive. Economically speaking, I suppose she was right: Love is free. When it comes to receiving love, especially God's love, there's nothing we can do to earn it. God is love, and God loves us whether we want it or not, at no expense to us.

But loving others is another matter. To follow Christ is to learn that love is costly, but it's a price worth paying.

Prep for the Journey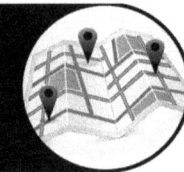

Agape is the Greek word that is often translated as love in the New Testament. "Agape love as modeled by Christ is not based on a feeling; rather, it is a determined act of the will, a joyful resolve to put the welfare of others above our own" (http://www.gotquestions.org/agape-love.html, October 19, 2015).

For humans, who tend to seek their own welfare first and foremost, this kind of love does not come naturally. The only way we are capable of showing this type of love is by having God's love flowing through us. Once we know God's love, we are able to love others as God loves us.

When has someone shown you agape love? When have you been able to show agape to someone else?

On the Road

Jesus said some pretty wild things concerning love. It's not surprising that his followers didn't always grasp what he was trying to tell them. He spoke about love in a radical way, using parables, metaphors, and other means to help those who would listen understand that love—the real, unconditional love of God about which he was teaching—is costly. Love requires giving.

Within John 3:16 (which is probably the most quoted verse in the New Testament) is a neon sign pointing to the cost of love.

Read John 3:16-17.

"For God so loved the world that he gave his only Son, so that everyone who believes in him may not perish but may have eternal life.

17"Indeed, God did not send the Son into the world to condemn the world, but in order that the world might be saved through him."

"For God so loved the world that he gave his only son…" Those words are a testament to the radical cost of love, but the context in which they were spoken gives us an even deeper look into just what it means to follow a revolutionary Messiah.

Jesus spoke these words to Nicodemus, a Jewish ruler and a Pharisee, who had come to see Jesus in secret. Nicodemus wanted to believe, but he was struggling to understand Jesus' radical teachings.

As a Pharisee, Nicodemus would have been steeped in the teachings of the Law of Moses, and the history of the Jewish people. The Law was a way of life for the people, affecting practically everything they did. For Nicodemus to consider setting aside all he had ever known to believe in Jesus must have been terrifying! But Nicodemus was obviously intrigued by Jesus' message.

Jesus spoke of God's love for the world—not just the Jews and the devout, but God's love for the world. For centuries the people of Israel had believed that God's love was only for those who were circumcised, Levitical law-abiding Jews. Jesus' message was (and is) for all who would listen. His promise of God's love, eternal life, and redemption for all people was blasphemy.

And it was this radical, blasphemous love that changed the heart even of Nicodemus the Pharisee. We see him again in John's Gospel, defending Jesus among the other religious rulers (John 7:50-52) and again after Jesus was crucified, bringing oils to anoint his body for burial (John 19:39-42).

When have you had a difficult time accepting God's unconditional love? Why?

How do Christians, well-meaning church people, behave like the Pharisees and limit God's love? What traditions and structures do we cling to more tightly than this radical, costly way of loving the world?

Scenic Route

What has being a follower of Christ cost you?

In Matthew's Gospel, shortly after calling the twelve disciples, Jesus warned them what following him would do to their lives. As Jesus delegated responsibilities to his disciples when he sent them to perform healings and declare the coming kingdom of heaven, he warned them that they would face persecution. He was sending them specifically to the Jews, those who had spent generations waiting to hear that the Messiah had come, but Jesus knew that many would hear, but not believe. The way Jesus came into the world and moved through it was not what Israel had expected of her Messiah. Because Jesus knew that he would be opposed, even to the point of death, he instructed the disciples not to expect any less for themselves. Following and proclaiming this love would eventually cost them their reputations, their families, and even their lives.

Read Matthew 10:26-38.

"So have no fear of them; for nothing is covered up that will not be uncovered, and nothing secret that will not become known. ²⁷What I say to you in the dark, tell in the light; and what you hear whispered, proclaim from the housetops. ²⁸Do not fear those who kill the body but cannot kill the soul; rather fear him who can destroy both soul and body in hell. ²⁹Are not two sparrows sold for a penny? Yet not one of them will fall to the ground apart from your Father. ³⁰And even the hairs of your head are all counted. ³¹So do not be afraid; you are of more value than many sparrows.

³²"Everyone therefore who acknowledges me before others, I also will acknowledge before my Father in heaven; ³³but whoever denies me before others, I also will deny before my Father in heaven.

³⁴"Do not think that I have come to bring peace to the earth; I have not come to bring peace, but a sword.

³⁵For I have come to set a man against his father,
and a daughter against her mother,
and a daughter-in-law against her mother-in-law;
³⁶and one's foes will be members of one's own household.
³⁷Whoever loves father or mother more than me is not worthy of me; and whoever loves son or daughter more than me is not worthy of me; ³⁸and whoever does not take up the cross and follow me is not worthy of me.

When we truly follow Christ, he must come before anyone or anything else. I doubt that even the disciples understood that— at least in the beginning. To those who did not understand or believe Jesus was the Messiah, his teachings must have sounded wrong on every level.

In what areas of your life do you have trouble putting Christ first?

Imagine telling your family, friends, and neighbors that everything for which they have been waiting is finally here. The God to whom they have been faithful has arrived in the flesh. God is with them and among them and loves them.

The disciples were among their own people, God's chosen people. But Jesus' teachings about love threatened everything they had been taught. Throughout their history, God had been their God and they had been God's people. It was thought to be an almost exclusive club.

The disciples put their lives on the line to spread Jesus' message. When they faced opposition from those whom they loved, they had to choose whether to speak the truth or be silent. Jesus promised that in their loss, in the cost of love, they would truly find life.

If we look at this passage in our own context, it would not be about going out into the world and evangelizing to people who are not Christians. Jesus sent the disciples to their own people, to the devout, and he promised that they would be met with opposition.

Where do you see the church hurting and opposing itself today?

Whom do you know who needs to hear the good news but isn't receptive to it? How can you share God's love with that person in a way that he or she might hear and believe?

Workers Ahead

The radical nature of God's love doesn't stop with religious people. In fact, God's radical love doesn't stop; it extends even to our enemies.

Read Luke 6:27-35.

"But I say to you that listen, Love your enemies, do good to those who hate you, 28bless those who curse you, pray for those who abuse you. 29If anyone strikes you on the cheek, offer the other also; and from anyone who takes away your coat do not withhold even your shirt. 30Give to everyone who begs from you; and if anyone takes away your goods, do not ask for them again. 31Do to others as you would have them do to you.

32"If you love those who love you, what credit is that to you? For even sinners love those who love them. 33If you do good to those who do good to you, what credit is that to you? For even sinners do the same. 34If you lend to those from whom you hope to receive, what credit is that to you? Even sinners lend to sinners, to receive as much again. 35But love your enemies, do good, and lend, expecting nothing in return. Your reward will be great, and you will be children of the Most High; for he is kind to the ungrateful and the wicked.

In Luke's Gospel, this call to love our enemies comes just after the Beatitudes through which Jesus completely turned the world's understanding of wealth, power, and privilege on its head. Loving our enemies is next on a long list that shows how different God's kingdom is from the broken world we know as reality.

How can you show love for your enemies? Talk with other members of the group about specific actions.

> What do you find most difficult about loving your enemies? How do you feel about our culture's need for a person to earn forgiveness?

Our culture tells us that the things we have are based on what we've earned and our willingness to work for them. In many instances, forgiveness must be earned. Justice has become about revenge rather than action that is life-giving. Love is reserved for those who are loving. But the culture of God's kingdom is the opposite of all we have built, trusted, and believed. The love of God gives—even to the worst among us, and as Christ's followers, we are commanded to do the same.

In the Rear View

Throughout his life and teachings, Jesus repeated a message of radical love so unlike anything his culture (or ours) understood that it is hard for many people to grasp it. At the same time, this radical love is so needed by those who acknowledge their brokenness that many choose to listen and to follow him. These radical teachings led to Jesus' arrest and death sentence. He paid the ultimate price for teaching and showing God's radical love.

Read John 13:1-5, 34-35.
Now before the festival of the Passover, Jesus knew that his hour had come to depart from this world and go to the Father. Having loved his own who were in the world, he loved them to the end. ²The devil had already put it into the heart of Judas son of Simon Iscariot to betray him. And during supper ³Jesus, knowing that the Father had given all things into his hands, and that he had come from God and was going to God, ⁴got up from the table, took off his outer robe, and tied a towel around himself. ⁵Then he poured water into a basin and began to wash the disciples' feet and to wipe them with the towel that was tied around him.
...
³⁴I give you a new commandment, that you love one another. Just as I have loved you, you also should love one another. ³⁵By this everyone will know that you are my disciples, if you have love for one another."

> How would your church change if it fully lived out this commandment to radical love? Consider individually, and as a group, how you can be an active part of that change.

Knowing that his time had come, Jesus reiterated his most important lesson for the disciples. He showed them that love is giving of one's self in service to others. Love is humbling one's self to care for the grimiest parts of the world. Love is giving up one's privilege and your power to wash the feet of people who have nothing to offer you. With Christ as our example, we are to show that radical love to one another.

Travel Log

Day 1:

Nicodemus was a devout man whose very way of life was threatened by Jesus' teachings. However, Nicodemus was brave enough to ask questions about this different love and life Jesus was calling him to follow. What questions do you have for Jesus? How would you explain this different love and life to someone who was not affiliated with Christianity? Note your responses to both questions in the space below.

Day 2:

Reflect on a time when someone tried to limit your love or God's love. What do you think was at the root of that struggle? How did it turn out in the end? Journal your reflections.

Day 3:

Whom do you identify as your enemies? (Enemies may be particular people, groups, institutions, or systems that threaten/oppose you, your communities, etc.) Make a list of these enemies. Then reread Luke 6:27-35. What would loving your enemies look like? Write a prayer for them today.

Day 4:

Consider the ways in which your culture (the nation, the church, etc.) opposes the type of radical love we see in Jesus' teachings. What do you see? From what you know about Christ's love, how do you think he would respond today? Note your responses below.

Day 5:
Write a prayer for your church's leaders and teachers, asking God to help them show radical love in all circumstances.

Day 6:
Reflect on your day (or week), looking for instances when you have seen the upside-down nature of Christ's love. When do you experience or see someone loving in a way that contradicts all common sense? Take note of these experiences.

Day 7:
Write a statement for what it means to you to love as Christ loves.

Love Isn't Always Pretty

Scripture for lesson:
Luke 10:38-42; John 11:1-46; 12:1-8

Written by Whitney Brown

My studio apartment is in a hundred year old house that is held together with plaster and a prayer. It looks, and often smells, as old as it is. There are at least ten quirks about the house that I tell guests upon their first visit. "Turn the lock and the handle at the same time to close the door. If the sink starts whistling, turn it on and off again."

Certainly, it's not the ideal place for hosting parties or having friends linger for a visit. It's not pretty, and it's not much, but it is my home; it's the space where I live; the space that contains the many things that make me who I am; and it's the space I want to share with my friends, especially when they need a couch on which to rest, a meal, or a listening ear. I try to make it as presentable as possible, but my first words, even to my most frequent visitors, are, "Sorry for the mess." But my friends don't come to enjoy an immaculate house; they come to spend time with me and with one another—to love and be loved—and love isn't always pretty.

Prep for the Journey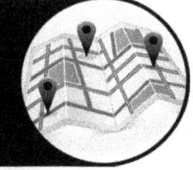

We don't always consider that Jesus had friends, especially outside of his disciples. The Bible doesn't give us many clues about his personal life as an adult, but he was human, and part of being human is having relationships with other people.

In the two stories used in this lesson, we learn that Jesus had a special relationship with a family who lived in Bethany. Siblings Mary, Martha, and Lazarus were more than just followers of Jesus; they were his friends. He went there when he needed time away from his ministry. We all need people with whom we can relax and "just be ourselves." In my opinion, Mary, Martha, and Lazarus were those kinds of friends to Jesus. It's also likely that Jesus stayed with these friends when he was in Jerusalem. Bethany was within walking distance of the city.

When do you find yourself apologizing for what you have to offer? Why?

How do you "get away from it all"? Who are the people with whom you can relax and be yourself? Why is it important to have such times?

How do you feel when people drop in unexpectedly? How do you react?

Are you a Mary or a Martha? How is your church like Martha? How is your church like Mary? What tasks are so pressing that they keep you from being truly present with the people you love?

On the Road

People have to be good friends just to drop in on one another, which is what it sounds like had happened in this passage from Luke. Can't you just see Martha bustling around the house, sending Lazarus for more wine, and quickly making more bread for their dinner?

Read Luke 10:38-42.

Now as they went on their way, he entered a certain village, where a woman named Martha welcomed him into her home. ³⁹She had a sister named Mary, who sat at the Lord's feet and listened to what he was saying. ⁴⁰But Martha was distracted by her many tasks; so she came to him and asked, "Lord, do you not care that my sister has left me to do all the work by myself? Tell her then to help me." ⁴¹But the Lord answered her, "Martha, Martha, you are worried and distracted by many things; ⁴²there is need of only one thing. Mary has chosen the better part, which will not be taken away from her."

Martha was concerned about the physical needs of her guests. Instead of helping with the preparations necessary to accommodate their guests, Mary sat down to talk with Jesus. Again I can see Martha, hands on her hips, hoping Jesus would chastise Mary for not helping her. Jesus instead commended Mary for doing the only thing that was needed. Just imagine Martha's shock and dismay at his rebuff!

My grandmother was a Martha. I remember her hovering around the table, asking what else we needed instead of joining us for the meal. Finally, my dad (her son) told her that all we needed was for her to sit down with us!

Scenic Route

John's Gospel tells of at least two times Jesus visited the home of Mary, Martha, and their brother, Lazarus, whom Jesus loved.

Read John 11:1-16.

Now a certain man was ill, Lazarus of Bethany, the village of Mary and her sister Martha. ²Mary was the one who anointed the Lord with perfume and wiped his feet with her hair; her brother Lazarus was ill. ³So the sisters sent a message to Jesus, "Lord, he whom you love is ill." ⁴But when Jesus heard it, he said, "This illness does not lead to death; rather it is for God's glory, so that the Son of God may be glorified through it." ⁵Accordingly, though Jesus loved Martha and her sister and Lazarus, ⁶after having heard that Lazarus was ill, he stayed two days longer in the place where he was. ⁷Then after this he said to the disciples, "Let us go to Judea again." ⁸The disciples said to him, "Rabbi, the Jews were just now trying to stone you, and are you going there again?" ⁹Jesus answered, "Are there not twelve hours of daylight? Those who walk during the day do not stumble, because they see the light of this world. ¹⁰But those who walk at night stumble, because the light is not in them." ¹¹After saying this, he told them, "Our friend Lazarus has fallen asleep, but I am going there to awaken him." ¹²The disciples said to him, "Lord, if he has fallen asleep, he will be all right." ¹³Jesus, however, had been speaking about his death, but they thought that he was referring merely to sleep. ¹⁴Then Jesus told them plainly, "Lazarus is dead. ¹⁵For your sake I am glad I was not there, so that you may believe. But let us go to him." ¹⁶Thomas, who was called the Twin, said to his fellow disciples, "Let us also go, that we may die with him."

Jesus loved Mary, Martha, and Lazarus, but he delayed his response to the sisters' message for two days. When he finally decided to head to Bethany, the disciples tried to persuade him to continue in the opposite direction. They had just come from Judea, where the Jews had tried to kill Jesus. What's more, Jesus had been foretelling his death and knew he was going to an area where he would be in greater danger. Though the disciples questioned Jesus' decision, they remained devoted and went with him, risking their own lives as well.

Read John 11:17-32.

When Jesus arrived, he found that Lazarus had already been in the tomb four days. ¹⁸Now Bethany was near Jerusalem, some two miles away, ¹⁹and many of the Jews had come to Martha and Mary to console them about their brother. ²⁰When Martha heard that Jesus was coming, she went and met him, while Mary stayed at home. ²¹Martha said to Jesus, "Lord, if you had been here, my brother would not have died. ²²But even now I know that God will give you whatever you ask of him." ²³Jesus said to her, "Your brother will rise again." ²⁴Martha said to him, "I know that he will rise again in the resurrection on the last day." ²⁵Jesus said to her, "I am the resurrection and the life. Those who believe in me, even though they die, will live, ²⁶and everyone who lives and believes in me will never die. Do you believe this?" ²⁷She said to him, "Yes, Lord, I believe that you are the Messiah, the Son of God, the one coming into the world." ²⁸When she had said this, she went back and called her sister Mary, and told her privately, "The Teacher is here and is calling for you." ²⁹And when she heard it, she got up quickly and went to him. ³⁰Now Jesus had not yet come to the village, but was still at the place where Martha had met him. ³¹The Jews who were with her in the house, consoling her, saw Mary get up quickly and go out. They followed her because they thought that she was going to the tomb to weep there. ³²When Mary came where Jesus was and saw him, she knelt at his feet and said to him, "Lord, if you had been here, my brother would not have died."

Lazarus was specifically mentioned as one whom Jesus loved. What does it mean to you to acknowledge that you are also one whom Jesus loves? How do you respond to this love?

> When have you had complete faith in God, despite circumstances that seemed to discredit that faith?

Martha and Mary fully believed that Jesus was the Messiah. Martha gave the first full profession of faith in the Gospel, and both sisters, through their actions, exhibited full faith and trust in Jesus despite their grief. Surrounded by neighbors, most of whom did not understand who Jesus was or believe what he was saying, the sisters reached out to the one they knew could heal their brother.

Read John 11:33-44.

When Jesus saw her weeping, and the Jews who came with her also weeping, he was greatly disturbed in spirit and deeply moved. ³⁴He said, "Where have you laid him?" They said to him, "Lord, come and see." ³⁵Jesus began to weep. ³⁶So the Jews said, "See how he loved him!" ³⁷But some of them said, "Could not he who opened the eyes of the blind man have kept this man from dying?" ³⁸Then Jesus, again greatly disturbed, came to the tomb. It was a cave, and a stone was lying against it. ³⁹Jesus said, "Take away the stone." Martha, the sister of the dead man, said to him, "Lord, already there is a stench because he has been dead four days." ⁴⁰Jesus said to her, "Did I not tell you that if you believed, you would see the glory of God?" ⁴¹So they took away the stone. And Jesus looked upward and said, "Father, I thank you for having heard me. ⁴²I knew that you always hear me, but I have said this for the sake of the crowd standing here, so that they may believe that you sent me." ⁴³When he had said this, he cried with a loud voice, "Lazarus, come out!" ⁴⁴The dead man came out, his hands and feet bound with strips of cloth, and his face wrapped in a cloth. Jesus said to them, "Unbind him, and let him go."

> Imagine yourself in this crowd. How might you have felt as you listened to Jesus prayer? when he commanded Lazarus to come out of the tomb? when Lazarus emerged?

Martha, ever the practical one, was hesitant to move the stone. Lazarus hadn't just died, but had been in the tomb for four days. The smell was so strong that it reached even outside the tomb, but a little stench didn't deter Jesus. He prayed, and in his prayer we learn that all of this was not just out of his great love for Mary, Martha, and Lazarus, but because he loved the people, he wanted all who witnessed the event to believe in him as the Messiah.

Read John 11:45-46.

Many of the Jews therefore, who had come with Mary and had seen what Jesus did, believed in him. ⁴⁶But some of them went to the Pharisees and told them what he had done.

It seems that one can't do a good deed without it causing problems! Jesus had just raised a man who had been dead for four days, but some people in the crowd were threatened by his actions. Jesus loved the people, but some of them weren't making it easy for Jesus. By running to the Pharisees to tell what had happened, they increased the religious leaders' resolve to kill Jesus.

> Whom do you call in your time of need? Who is in the crowd that surrounds you when you are hurting?

Workers Ahead

There is ample evidence to suggest that this story of Mary anointing Jesus' feet is either a mixture of details from other accounts or one that a later editor added. Luke 5:36-50 tells of a woman of questionable reputation who came to where Jesus was dining and stood behind him as she waited to anoint him. Her tears fell on his feet, and she wiped them away with her hair and then anointed his feet. Women of her ilk were known to wear their hair unbound.

Mary, as a lady of the house, would not have worn her hair loose. To have wiped the perfumed oil away with her hair would have been completely unacceptable. It would also have been very strange for Mary to have poured the perfume on Jesus' feet rather than his head. Some sources suggest that the gift was given in appreciation for Jesus having raised Lazarus from the dead.

Read John 12:1-8.

Six days before the Passover Jesus came to Bethany, the home of Lazarus, whom he had raised from the dead. ²There they gave a dinner for him. Martha served, and Lazarus was one of those at the table with him. ³Mary took a pound of costly perfume made of pure nard, anointed Jesus' feet, and wiped them with her hair. The house was filled with the fragrance of the perfume. ⁴But Judas Iscariot, one of his disciples (the one who was about to betray him), said, ⁵"Why was this perfume not sold for three hundred denarii and the money given to the poor?" ⁶(He said this not because he cared about the poor, but because he was a thief; he kept the common purse and used to steal what was put into it.) ⁷Jesus said, "Leave her alone. She bought it so that she might keep it for the day of my burial. ⁸You always have the poor with you, but you do not always have me."

Jesus returned to Bethany one more time. Martha, of course, served dinner, and Mary was again at Jesus' feet. This time she was not just listening. She made a grand gesture in an outpouring of love by anointing Jesus. Mary seemed to understand that Jesus would not be with them much longer. She wanted to show her love for Jesus while he was still present.

Mary's gift represented about a year's wages for a laborer, which was quite extravagant. However, when we love someone, the cost of showing that love may not be a primary consideration.

Mary and Martha both showed their love for Jesus through their actions, even though their actions were very different. Jesus also showed his love for these friends, and for others, through his actions.

How do you show your love to others? In your opinion, what is the most important way to show your love? How will you be more intentional in showing love to all people?

In the Rear View

When we love someone, we want to get it right. From love songs to romantic comedies and even the fairy tales we tell our children, we paint a perfect, pretty picture of love, and we try to live up to those expectations. These unrealistic expectations often do more to drive a wedge between us in our attempts to love one another than to amplify that love. Whether it's the expectations we have for ourselves or those we have of our loved ones that are unmet, we believe that a less-than-perfect picture means something is lacking in our love.

These stories show us that love is often messy. The condition of the house is less important than being present with your guests. Love means being present for people even when things are not pretty. It's during those times that we show love to those around us.

What unrealistic expectations of love do you have?

Travel Log

Day 1:

From Luke's story of Martha and Mary, we learn that even necessary, routine acts can keep us from being truly devoted to God. True devotion and love require times to be still, listen, and worship. Write down a simple outline of your daily schedule. Note where you can "find" the time for these important elements of your life. Make a point of implementing these schedule changes.

Day 2:

Jesus came to his friends in a time of loss and grieved alongside them. Even surrounded by people we love, grief can often cause us to feel alone. This story reminds us that God is present in our grief and trials, and shares deeply in our burdens. Journal about a time when you have experienced God's presence when you felt alone.

Day 3:

Loving others means serving them. What gifts do you have? How can you use your gifts to show love to another person? List your gifts. Beside each gift, write one way in which you can use that gift to show love to another person.

Day 4:

By the time Jesus reached Bethany, Lazarus had been dead for four days. When have you reached out to God and found the answer to be slower or different than you wanted or expected? Write some of your thoughts, feelings, and frustrations about that experience.

Day 5:
    When have you had an attempt to do something positive, something loving, used against you? How has that incident kept you from making more attempts? Write down your thoughts about what happened. Sometimes writing down troubling things helps us to gain a different perspective.

Day 6:
    We all have friends or family members with whom we have neglected to stay in touch. Just as Mary realized that Jesus would not be with them much longer, your friends and family will not be with you forever. List those people with whom you have lost touch or have not contacted recently. Pick up the phone and call some of them today.

Day 7:
Reflect on a time in your life when loving someone, or allowing someone to love you, was difficult. What positive outcomes do you see now? Write down some of your thoughts.

Love that Changes Everything

Scripture for lesson:
Matthew 27:57-60; Mark 15:42-47

Written by Whitney Brown

People respond in many different ways when someone dies. Some people immediately organize a group to provide food for the family. Others stop to call or visit with the family, wondering how to offer comfort. Some people will order flowers or express their love and concern in other ways.

As families make funeral arrangements, a vast array of things often come into play. Maybe there are feelings of remorse or guilt over a strained relationship with the person who died, or maybe there is pressure from other family members to do things a certain way. If the person's body is to be buried, the funeral director may exert some not-so-subtle influence about the choice of a casket and vault. There is the service to be planned. Should it be a somber time of mourning or an opportunity to celebrate the life of the deceased one? What happens if the person does not already own a cemetery plot?

All of these decisions come when people are least equipped to deal with them. Even if the person's death has been expected for some time, it is still difficult to deal with the reality when it happens. While trying to make these decisions, the family is also grieving. They want to do right by their loved one, but finances and other issues may be the difference between what they want to do and the choices they actually make.

> What do you do when someone dies? How do you offer comfort and support?

Prep for the Journey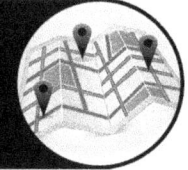

Although all four Gospels tell about Joseph of Arimathea, this lesson will use only the texts from Matthew and Mark. Other than the ones associated with the Last Supper and Jesus' death and resurrection, only five events are recorded in all four Gospels, which tells us how important this story is.

Each of the Gospel writers likely had a different purpose or audience in mind when he recorded the life of Jesus and his teachings.

> How does knowing that this story is told in all four Gospels affect the way you view it?

Matthew targeted a Jewish audience. He began by establishing Jesus' Jewish heritage all the way back to Moses. By so doing, he was setting the scene to prove Jesus was the long-awaited Messiah.

Scholars disagree as to whether Matthew or Mark was written first, but it has become increasingly more accepted that Mark predates Matthew's writing. Mark was organized chronologically, as much as was possible. Many of the events, and even some of the wording, from Mark's Gospel appear in Matthew and in Luke to some extent. Written after the mass persecution of Christians began, Mark's purpose was "intensely practical. He was writing a book for the guidance and support of his fellow Christians in a situation of intense crisis" (*The Interpreter's Bible, Vol. 7*, page 633-34, © 1951).

In all the Gospel accounts, it is only after Jesus was crucified that we hear the name of Joseph of Arimathea. He had not been a prominent character until this point. In fact, John's account of this story says that Joseph was a secret follower because he was afraid of the Jewish leaders. However, this obscure follower stepped into the dangerous spotlight when everyone else was in hiding. Joseph approached Pilate, who had ordered Jesus' crucifixion, and asked for the body so that he might honor his Messiah.

> When do you hesitate to claim Jesus as the Messiah? Why?

On the Road

As you may recall from the story of Jesus raising Lazarus from death (previous lesson), Jesus and his disciples were going to Jerusalem where they would celebrate the Passover. For those who lived close enough to make the journey, Passover was to be observed in Jerusalem. Less than a week before, Jesus had been welcomed into the city with shouts of Hosanna.

After partaking of the Passover meal, Jesus tried once more to tell his disciples what was about to happen, but they did not yet understand. He told them that they would all desert him, but they could not even comprehend that possibility.

> When have you had difficulty making someone understand what you were trying to communicate? How did you feel when, despite your best efforts, they still "didn't get it"?

In Mark's account of Jesus' arrest and crucifixion, we see the Messiah suffering alone, surrounded only by his enemies, while a few of his followers watched from a safe distance. The following passage picks up right after Jesus' death.

Read Mark 15:42-47.

When evening had come, and since it was the day of Preparation, that is, the day before the sabbath, ⁴³Joseph of Arimathea, a respected member of the council, who was also himself waiting expectantly for the kingdom of God, went boldly to Pilate and asked for the body of

Jesus. ⁴⁴Then Pilate wondered if he were already dead; and summoning the centurion, he asked him whether he had been dead for some time. ⁴⁵When he learned from the centurion that he was dead, he granted the body to Joseph. ⁴⁶Then Joseph bought a linen cloth, and taking down the body, wrapped it in the linen cloth, and laid it in a tomb that had been hewn out of the rock. He then rolled a stone against the door of the tomb. ⁴⁷Mary Magdalene and Mary the mother of Joses saw where the body was laid.

Jewish custom was to bury people the same day they died. While the Roman authorities might have left Jesus' body on the cross as food for vultures, it was against Jewish law to leave bodies hanging overnight. The Jews would probably have given him some sort of burial, but not with the love and care Joseph showed.

Joseph himself removed Jesus' body from the cross, wrapped it, and carried it to a tomb. For Joseph to have approached Pilate to ask for the body of Jesus, who was considered to have been a heretic, indicates that Joseph clearly cared for and cherished Jesus. In addition to grieving the loss of Jesus, who was likely a friend and mentor, Joseph saw the horrific condition of his body as he removed him from the cross. Joseph touched his wounds, wrapped his body for burial, and placed him in a tomb. In Mark's account, we find Joseph walking through this alone, just as Jesus walked through his final trials alone.

When have you seen the church respond in love like Joseph—being present in grief, stepping up when others turn away, tending to the needs of the broken and abandoned? When have you seen the church respond like the disciples in Mark—deserting at the time of greatest need? When have you deserted during a time of great need?

Scenic Route

Matthew's Gospel also mentions Joseph of Arimathea. In Matthew, we learn a little more about this man who gave Jesus a proper burial.

Read Matthew 27:57-60.

When it was evening, there came a rich man from Arimathea, named Joseph, who was also a disciple of Jesus. ⁵⁸He went to Pilate and asked for the body of Jesus; then Pilate ordered it to be given to him. ⁵⁹So Joseph took the body and wrapped it in a clean linen cloth ⁶⁰and laid it in his own new tomb, which he had hewn in the rock. He then rolled a great stone to the door of the tomb and went away.

As in Mark's account, Matthew says that Joseph asked Pilate for Jesus' body. He then prepared the body for burial and put it in a tomb. However, Matthew says Joseph was a known follower of Jesus. The tomb where he laid Jesus was his own new tomb, and Joseph had hewn it in the rock himself.

Matthew referred to Joseph as being rich. The word translated as "rich" could also have meant honorable or respected. Since wealth had a lot to do with one's status in the community, it's quite possible that all of those terms applied to Joseph. This was no doubt a more extravagant burial than any other crucified criminals received. Joseph went to great expense to give Jesus an honorable and proper burial.

The rich are warned throughout Jesus' teachings that following him will be hard for them. The Twelve were asked to leave all they had to journey with Jesus. People who have a lot of wealth and possessions can allow those things to distract them and distort their vision from the true source of power and love. Jesus did not say it was wrong to be wealthy, but he did warn against the dangers of treasuring your wealth. Many times we focus more on the followers of Jesus who lived on the margins of society, but there were also a few noted wealthy followers. Joseph was one such man, and this story of Jesus' burial shows us how he used his wealth in a valuable way—a way that changes the course of Christian history.

Instead of Jesus' body being taken down with the other criminals and put into an unmarked grave, he was placed with care and religious rites into a well-marked tomb. His followers would have known where to find his body (or so they thought).

Having a distinct tomb was important to the rest of the story. Knowing exactly where Jesus was buried, in this uniquely hewn tomb, well-marked as belonging to Joseph of Arimathea, was key in knowing that Jesus was not there three days later. After all, how could his followers claim resurrection if they weren't exactly sure where his body had been placed? Because Joseph had given Jesus such a special "final" resting place, the disciples knew where to go to pay their respects and to grieve together. If Jesus had been put in an unmarked grave, not only would it have been a religious disgrace and dishonor, but no one would have been sure where to find the body. Our story would be completely different.

Workers Ahead

Joseph put his privilege and power to good use. Perhaps it was Joseph's status that made him the best candidate for such a task; a rich, respected member of either a local religious council or possibly of the Sanhedrin would not have been dismissed as easily as the rag-tag bunch of misfits who had been following Jesus throughout the countryside. But Joseph also had a lot to lose by being a known associate of this group.

Whether we realize it or not, each of us has an area of influence—a type of privilege and power. We have groups of friends, are members of organizations, participate in community events, and so

---

When have you seen people with more disposable income than other people treated differently in the church? How might the church address that situation?

What things distract you from your relationship with Jesus?

What are you willing to do for Jesus? How will the story of Christianity be different because of your actions?

What are your areas of influence? How can you use your influence to show love to others? Think in specific terms.

forth. All of those things bring us into contact with other people, which provides opportunities to influence them to support programs, change laws, fund initiatives, etc. As we work on behalf of others, we are showing love for Jesus.

In the Rear View

The brief glimpse we have of Joseph of Arimathea is one of the most intimate expressions of love in the Gospels. Though we are not given many details, we can imagine the heartbreak Joseph must have experienced when Jesus was crucified. Then, amidst the grief, come the responsibilities of caring for the person's physical body and making the necessary preparations. The grief surrounding such preparations is taxing enough as we balance grief and the necessity to make plans and gather family.

The hope of the resurrection, that Jesus has left this tomb and is indeed alive, is the key to our faith. Joseph of Arimathea's risky devotion is one of the many ways love plays into this story. Joseph was present when others fled, and his love for Jesus was evident in the intimacy of his actions.

May we love Jesus so intimately as to care for the lonely and hurting among us in a way that changes their story—and ours.

What resources does your church possess? Think of material possessions, as well as gifts, talents, and programs your church community offers. What are the greatest needs you see in the surrounding community? How can your church's resources help meet those needs? What are the risks you take in offering that help? What examples do you see in your own church or other churches where such resources are already at work? What difference are the church's resources making in your community? In what areas will you commit to exerting some influence?

Travel Log

Day 1:

Write the story of Jesus' crucifixion from the point of view of Joseph of Arimathea. What was he feeling when he approached Pilate? Was he angry because none of the other followers had stepped up for this task? What reactions did he anticipate from friends and family?

Day 2:

When has someone unexpected stepped up to help when you needed it most? Write a few words or sentences about that experience. Include your thoughts and feelings.

Day 3:
Think about a time when you were able to be present with someone or help in some way when no one else could or would reach out to them. What changed in your life and theirs through that experience? Write a prayer of thanks for the opportunity to show God's love in that situation.

Day 4:
Some of our most difficult experiences are during times of intense grief following the loss of a loved one. Death and dying are sacred experiences for people on all sides. Reflect on a funeral you attended that stands out in your mind when you consider these things. What made it special? Journal about your feelings regarding death and dying.

Day 5:

In Mark's account, the disciples fled when Jesus was arrested. They were not present through his trial or torture, nor at his death. Although they had plenty of reasons to be afraid for their own lives, a crucifixion would have been difficult to witness as it was a particularly brutal death. Still, there is no doubt they would have felt remorse for leaving when Jesus needed them most. There would have been things they had wanted to say and plenty of regrets. Write a letter to a deceased loved one using words you wish you had said more often, or maybe things you failed to say. Alternately, write a prayer from the perspective of the disciples in this story.

Day 6:

Visit the "final" resting place of someone. This could be someone you love or even a stranger. If this visit takes you to a cemetery, pause to read about and honor those who are buried nearby. Consider the love family and friends had for those who are buried there, as well as the love shown to family and friends by the deceased. Make a list of words you see.

Day 7:
    Because Jesus' trial and crucifixion was so horrific, we don't like to linger on that story. We also know how the story ends, so we like to skip ahead to the happy part. We often miss moments like this intimate burial story and the love shown by Joseph of Arimathea. Intentionally slow down today. Put aside your struggles and other things for a while. What intimacy is calling for your attention? Whose love are you missing? What changes will you make so as to share that love? Make some notes below.

Love Is a Verb

Scripture for lesson:
John 21:2-3, 15-24

Written by Whitney Brown

Have you ever found yourself overcome with road rage? For me it happens more often in the grocery store aisle than in traffic. I don't yell at other shoppers, but in my mind there is an almost constant groan as I try to navigate around unattended carts, understocked shelves, and the lady with twenty coupons who is checking out ahead of me. Shopping/driving/working would all be much more pleasant, at times, without people.

Even the kindest among us struggle to deal with people from time to time. It doesn't bring us much comfort to be reminded that we have to love them. A sweet, southern, "Bless your heart," might sound kind, but it doesn't really put into action the type of love we are commanded to share. Yet, even knowing we will fall short, God repeatedly calls us to love. Jesus taught that love means action. In other words, love is a verb. We see the truth of this statement throughout Jesus' teachings. He reinforced this truth with the disciples, even after his resurrection.

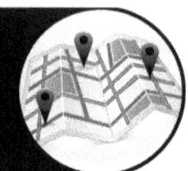

Prep for the Journey

What joy! Jesus was alive! The tomb was empty, and he had appeared to the disciples just as he said he would. According to the Gospel of John, Jesus appeared to the larger group of disciples twice, both times while they were behind locked doors. After all, the Jewish religious leaders had branded Jesus as a heretic and arranged to have him killed. What was to keep them from doing the same to the disciples?

Just imagine yourself in the disciples' position. Their leader had been crucified as a common criminal, but they believed he had risen from the dead. "They had seen the risen Lord; they had been given audacious promises by him; they had again been called to a high service for him and the world. Yet day crept after day and nothing happened" (*The Interpreter's Bible, Vol. 8*, page 803, © 1952).

How do you treat love as a verb?

When have you found yourself without purpose or direction? What did you do? What helped you to find purpose and direction?

With no specific purpose or direction, the disciples were reduced to idleness. Having nothing to do can really put a strain on people, especially when there is already a lot of confusion and stress. Finally, Peter had had enough. He was a man of action, and he decided to take action! What did he decide to do? Go fishing, of course.

Read John 21:2-3.

Gathered there together were Simon Peter, Thomas called the Twin, Nathanael of Cana in Galilee, the sons of Zebedee, and two others of the disciples. ³Simon Peter said to them, "I am going fishing." They said to him, "We will go with you." They went out and got into the boat, but that night they caught nothing.

Their decision made perfect sense for them. They were returning to what they knew how to do. It was not what they thought Jesus had been telling them, what he had been teaching them, but doing something was better than not doing anything.

The disciples had fished all night without any success. At dawn, a man on the shore shouted to them, telling them to put their net on the other side of the boat. When they did, they caught more fish than they could carry. As the sun continued to rise, the disciple whom Jesus loved recognized Jesus as the man on shore. Upon learning that the man was Jesus, Simon Peter impetuously jumped out of the boat and swam to shore. He left the others to struggle with the huge catch. When everyone arrived on the shore, Jesus already had a fire going and a breakfast of fish and bread prepared.

Read John 21:15-17.

When they had finished breakfast, Jesus said to Simon Peter, "Simon son of John, do you love me more than these?" He said to him, "Yes, Lord; you know that I love you." Jesus said to him, "Feed my lambs." ¹⁶A second time he said to him, "Simon son of John, do you love me?" He said to him, "Yes, Lord; you know that I love you." Jesus said to him, "Tend my sheep." ¹⁷He said to him the third time, "Simon son of John, do you love me?" Peter felt hurt because he said to him the third time, "Do you love me?" And he said to him, "Lord, you know everything; you know that I love you." Jesus said to him, "Feed my sheep."

The last time this group had shared a meal, Judas left abruptly, going to betray Jesus. Jesus had known his death was imminent and told the disciples that they could not yet go where he was going. After that declaration, Peter claimed that he would follow Jesus and lay down

---

How do you deal with idleness? What have you seen happen as the result of idleness?

When you don't know what action to take, do you remain as you are or move forward? Why?

What causes you to act impetuously? How do you feel when other people act impetuously, especially when they leave you with a bigger share of the work?

When have you made a promise without knowing what would be required to fulfill that promise? Did you keep the promise? Why or why not? How did that experience affect your willingness to commit to things?

When have you disappointed someone to the point that you were in utter despair? How were you able to repair the relationship? What had to happen before you could forgive yourself?

As followers of Jesus, we are uniquely both sheep and shepherds. We are a part of the flock in need of tending, and we are also called to do the work of the shepherd. How do we work together to balance these roles and allow them to exist simultaneously?

his life for him. Peter was always quick to jump into things, even when he had no idea what was involved. Jesus knew that before the next day began, Peter would deny even knowing him—not just once, but three times (John 13:36-38).

It was by a fire much like the one warming them during this breakfast that Peter had denied Jesus and heard the rooster crow (John 18:17, 25-27). It's fitting, then, that Jesus used a miracle and a meal to bring the disciples together and renew his relationship with them—especially with Peter.

We can only imagine Peter's remorse and humiliation when he realized that he had indeed denied Jesus three times. As Jesus repeated his question to Peter, it could almost have felt like harassment. Peter was obviously repentant, so why was Jesus belaboring the point?

Jesus' questions to Peter show the standard by which Jesus judges all of us: love. Peter had to forgive himself so that he could show to others the love about which Jesus had taught. Loving Jesus would require work, because love requires action. We are to use those actions to show love to others.

Scenic Route

In John 10, Jesus described himself as the "good shepherd." A good shepherd speaks with a voice the sheep recognize and understand, using calls and movements that instruct them to safety and good pasture. Good shepherds put themselves between their sheep and all danger. The health and welfare of the sheep is the sole concern of the good shepherd. In these verses, Jesus recalled that imagery for Peter, explaining that loving Jesus means loving his sheep. Peter was to be a good shepherd, caring for the sheep, risking his life for them, instructing them, and leading them as Jesus has done. If Peter wanted to love Jesus and lay down his life for him as he claimed, the way to do so was to show this deep love for the ones Jesus loved.

The charge for those who love Jesus is to act on that love and to, in turn, love one another (John 13). Proclaiming love for Jesus cannot be separated from the call to care for his sheep. This call to Peter, and Peter's fulfillment of it, is a call and a witness to all who choose to follow and love Jesus.

Read John 21:18-24.
Very truly, I tell you, when you were younger, you used to fasten your own belt and to go wherever you wished. But when you grow old, you will stretch out your hands, and someone else will fasten a belt around you and take you where you do not wish to go." [19](He said this

to indicate the kind of death by which he would glorify God.) After this he said to him, "Follow me."

[20]Peter turned and saw the disciple whom Jesus loved following them; he was the one who had reclined next to Jesus at the supper and had said, "Lord, who is it that is going to betray you?" [21]When Peter saw him, he said to Jesus, "Lord, what about him?" [22]Jesus said to him, "If it is my will that he remain until I come, what is that to you? Follow me!" [23]So the rumor spread in the community that this disciple would not die. Yet Jesus did not say to him that he would not die, but, "If it is my will that he remain until I come, what is that to you?" [24]This is the disciple who is testifying to these things and has written them, and we know that his testimony is true.

In his usual strange way with metaphors and imagery, Jesus told Peter what was in store for him as he lived out his life following Jesus. The Book of Acts tells of many of the works Peter performed and the struggles he faced. We know from other ancient texts and church tradition that Peter (and many other early followers of Jesus) died as martyrs for their faith, crucified just like Jesus.

Seeing "the disciple whom Jesus loved," Peter inquired about what would happen to him. Jesus called Peter to focus on his own path and follow him. We learn that this beloved disciple would live and share the story of all he had witnessed. This disciple's call was to share and to write, just as Peter's call was to follow and share by teaching and preaching.

Jesus affirmed both of these calls in this passage. Whether teaching through spoken words, going to dangerous places, writing the things you are shown, or through any host of other actions, God calls us all to love and to follow. Whatever gifts you have, whatever way you are called to use those gifts, your particular call is just as necessary and blessed as the highest call you can imagine. Our instructions are to follow and to love as Christ loved—with action.

Workers Ahead

Jesus gave Peter very specific instructions as to how to show his love for him—care for the sheep. We have the same instructions. This command is not just for those sheep who are like us, but for all of God's sheep, which is an overwhelming task. However, Jesus didn't say we had to do it by ourselves. He is with us as we minister, helping us to use the gifts and abilities of one another to fulfill this calling.

Your group is also part of the flock, each person having unique gifts and calls, with many still in the process of discerning their gifts. Affirm the gifts and calls of the people present in your group.

People will sometimes express the desire to know what the future holds. Jesus gave Peter some indication of what was to come. Would you want to know what the future will bring? Why or why not?

What things have you felt God calling you to do? Where have you felt God calling you to go? What types of calls do we tend to place "higher" than others? Why?

How is Jesus calling you to feed his flock? How is he calling your group and your faith community to feed his flock? How are you responding to that call?

Work together to compile a list of the needs within your flock, starting with those of the people in your small group. Broaden the list to include your faith community. Look beyond the church and into your local community and then to the nation and the world. Think of those who are unable to leave their homes or are in nursing homes or hospitals, those who are grieving, those who are seeking work, those who are battling or recovering from addiction, those who are caregivers for aging family members, those who don't have shelter, those who cannot read, and so forth. The list could become overwhelming, so choose only a couple of areas on which to concentrate, but keep the list. Refer to it from time to time, choosing additional ways through which to tend the sheep.

In the Rear View

As Christians, God calls each of us to love and care for other people: neighbors, people who have been hurtful to us, the community of believers, the rude driver or grocery shopper, and even ourselves. This work is more than enough to keep us busy for eternity!

As we work to affirm and love one another, we can also be encouraged that the many different calls God gives to each of us are valuable to God's kingdom. Discerning our gifts and calls and seeking to use them for God's glory are important steps in helping us become better shepherds. The community of faith in which we find ourselves is the flock on which we can depend to help us in our journey of showing love to all of God's sheep.

When Jesus asks, "Do you love me?" will your words match your actions?

Travel Log

Day 1:

I know that my patience with people runs out faster when I am in a hurry or when what they're doing interferes with my rhythm or my plan. A loud, busy grocery store is where my kindness and patience go to die. Slowing down and acknowledging the humanity around me helps me to love even the most annoying shoppers.

When or where do you find your patience with people stretched to the limit? How can you manage to show love to the people in those situations or places? Jot down some ideas below.

Day 2:

Twice, Jesus told Peter, "Feed my sheep." There are many in the world whose basic needs, like food and shelter, are not met. Make a list of organizations, including the Cumberland Presbyterian Church, who work to provide basic needs for people. How can you support the efforts of these organizations? How do these kinds of efforts show love?

Day 3:

Make a list with three columns. In the first, write the names of the people you see every day. In the second and third, answer these questions: What needs do those people have in their lives right now? What actions can you take to care for them and show them love?

Day 4:

What are your gifts? These may be particular talents or skills you possess, or it could be part of your disposition (joy, mercy, compassion, practicality, etc.). If you have trouble answering this question, ask someone who knows you well what they think.

Day 5:

Pray for a young person you know. Children, teens, and young adults are in formative and transformative stages in life where they are still determining who they want to be in this world. (Sometimes we find ourselves asking that same question as adults, too.) Write down some of the specific things for which you will pray. Refer back to your notes after a few weeks. Look for any changes in the person's faith journey.

Day 6:

When Jesus returned, he went to his friends to reassure them of his love and presence with them as he sent them out into the world, empowered and encouraged to do the work he had called them to do. How does Jesus' faithful presence with you, even in your times of wandering, empower and encourage you? Write a letter to Jesus, thanking him for the encouragement and sharing any concerns you have about what he is calling you to do.

Day 7:
   Who are the sheep in your flock? How are you faithfully caring for them? Identify either individuals or groups of people. Write down one or two words that indicate how you are being a good shepherd. If you find that you have not been as good a shepherd to some members of your flock, note some ideas as to how you can improve.

Love as the Way

Scripture for lesson:
1 Corinthians 13

Written by Tiffany Hall McClung

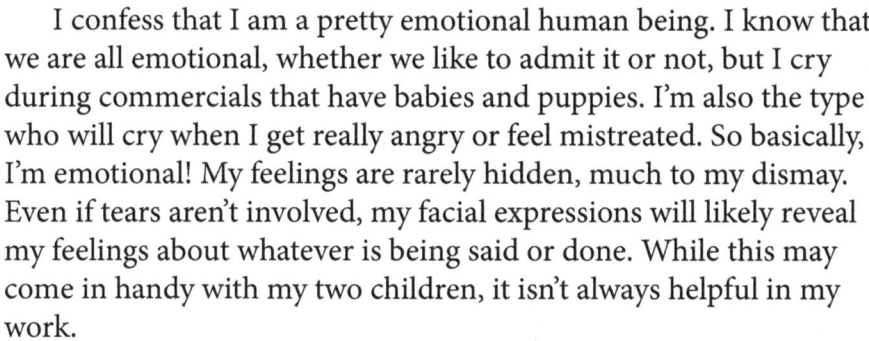

I confess that I am a pretty emotional human being. I know that we are all emotional, whether we like to admit it or not, but I cry during commercials that have babies and puppies. I'm also the type who will cry when I get really angry or feel mistreated. So basically, I'm emotional! My feelings are rarely hidden, much to my dismay. Even if tears aren't involved, my facial expressions will likely reveal my feelings about whatever is being said or done. While this may come in handy with my two children, it isn't always helpful in my work.

Our emotions are gifts from God, mysterious gifts that I won't claim to understand any more than I can control. Emotions can also be misleading and dangerous when we fail to pair them with our intellects. For example, when one of my children says, "I don't feel like doing my homework." I absolutely believe that he or she is experiencing a true emotion that brings forth all kinds of other feelings, which leads to the desire to skip homework. Rather than responding, "Okay baby. I know your feeling is real, so let's just put that homework aside for now until you feel like doing it," I am more likely to say, "Well, I'm sorry. We often have to do things we don't feel like doing. Now, get it done!"

> How well can you control your emotions? How do you see your emotions as gifts from God?

Prep for the Journey

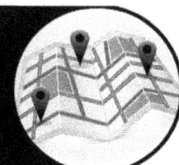

The scripture for this lesson is from what has become known as "The Love Chapter." Many people will know a lot of chapter 13 by heart because they have heard it so often. It makes a beautiful passage for a wedding, especially when moving into the second section of the chapter: "Love is patient; love is kind" and all that. We have wrapped this short thirteen-versed chapter in a pretty red bow, written "Love" on it, and given it to ourselves as a big emotional gift. Unfortunate-

> How familiar are you with 1 Corinthians 13? When have you heard it used most frequently? What would be other appropriate uses?

> This chapter of First Corinithians may be the passage of scripture most often used in weddings. Having learned what we have, how do you imagine this became so? Was it used at your own wedding? In what ways would it still be very appropriate for a wedding within the proper context?

> What levels of hierarchy exist within your congregation—if not about the spiritual gifts that Paul mentions, then what? How can you work together to create love as a framework for all that is done? How would love correct those places of comparison, competition, and emotion?

ly, the Apostle Paul, who wrote the letters to this church in Corinth, never intended it as such.

Paul founded the Corinthian church in the midst of a city that was extremely diverse. Naturally, the make-up of this early Christian church mirrored the diversity of the city. The new converts were most likely Gentiles who had converted from pagan religious practices to Christianity after listening to Paul. As the new church grew, small groups of people met in different quadrants of the city to share a common meal and worship. At this point, Paul felt confident enough to leave the Corinthians and continue the business of planting new churches.

After having left Corinth for other areas, Paul received word that the church in Corinth was completely falling apart. The diversity that Paul had deemed a positive attribute was now threatening to undermine all of his hard work. When the small groups met, the people started comparing themselves based on the spiritual gifts about which Paul had taught them, creating a hierarchy of the spiritual gifts. That issue was the one that truly grated on Paul's nerves, so he wrote a letter to try to correct the situation until he could get back to Corinth to teach them again.

Read 1 Corinthians 12:31–13:3.

But strive for the greater gifts. And I will show you a still more excellent way. ¹If I speak in the tongues of mortals and of angels, but do not have love, I am a noisy gong or a clanging cymbal. ² And if I have prophetic powers, and understand all mysteries and all knowledge, and if I have all faith, so as to remove mountains, but do not have love, I am nothing. ³ If I give away all my possessions, and if I hand over my body so that I may boast, but do not have love, I gain nothing.

For Paul, the exhortation regarding love was meant to correct the Corinthians' assumption that some spiritual gifts were better than others. Love does not become the most important gift, but provides a framework within which all the spiritual gifts exist. It is a way of being, not a feel-good emotion.

The section of scripture above includes the final verse of chapter 12. Paul ended the section he had written about spiritual gifts by saying, "but strive for the greater gifts." Paul was not going to fall into the trap of placing one spiritual gift over another, letting the people know that their squabbling was absolutely ridiculous. From there, he took apart any arguments the people raised had for importance of any particular gift. Through a brilliant use of rhetoric, Paul put all the gifts (and, therefore, the gifted) on the same level. "You say that you speak in tongues and that makes you feel superior? Well, I'm telling you that you aren't acting very loving, so you are nothing but a lot of noise and hot air."

On the Road

In Romans 2:4, another letter written by Paul, the Apostle described God as "patient and kind." As he began to personify love in the selection below, also from Corinthians, these are the first two qualities used to point the reader toward agape. It is important to note that Paul does not mention Christ in this chapter. One scholar, Richard B. Hays, says, "Agape is presented here as a quality or character attribute that is to be shown forth in the action of members of the church." In other words, Christ may not be mentioned, but living as Christ is understood.

Read 1 Corinthians 13:4-7.

Love is patient; love is kind; love is not envious or boastful or arrogant⁵ or rude. It does not insist on its own way; it is not irritable or resentful; ⁶ it does not rejoice in wrongdoing, but rejoices in the truth. ⁷ It bears all things, believes all things, hopes all things, endures all things.

After quickly setting up what love is—patient and kind—Paul immediately pointed out all the ways the congregation was living contrary to those virtues. It is no coincindence that each of the "love is not…" statements corresponds to a behavior that Paul had already rebuked in earlier parts of the letter. If there was ever a question about what the Corinthians were up to that disappointed Paul so much, one needs look no further than the list in these verses: love is not envious, boastful, arrogant, rude, irritable, resentful, nor does it insist on its own way or rejoice when others hurt.

Paul used this short section of "The Love Chapter" to teach the Corinthians that love is not an emotion that comes and goes. Instead, love is an action and a way of living in the world—when we feel like it and when we don't. It wasn't enough for Paul to have Corinthians understand that the love of which he wrote was not an emotional feeling. The Corinthians needed to comprehend that love is active, and the actions performed in the name of love keep everything else in perspective. Paul made that concept clear in verse seven: "It bears all things, believes all things, hopes all things, endures all things."

Scenic Route

If it wasn't already clear that this chapter of Paul's letter is not a love poem, or a poem about love, the final verses of the chapter

> In what ways do you exhibit active love? How does your church enact this principle? Be specific, and attempt to look beyond the "easy answers." In what ways does knowing what love is not help you to better understand what love is? Where do you see that kind of love around you?

offer significant clarification. Paul was writing to a congregation who seems to have lost sight of the big picture. Instead of focusing on the whole congregation, they were squabbling between and within their small groups. Rather than celebrating the provision of God's many gifts to the diverse community, they created a hierarchy so as to compare one gift with the next. They also did not place their spiritual gifts in the proper context of the community of faith. Individuals seemed to have believed particular gifts provided them immediate and better access to God's kingdom. In order to correct these views, Paul stated simply, "Love never ends," before proceeding to explain that every spiritual gift a person may have—while good, useful, and truly a gift from God—will only last for a time in the bigger picture of eternity.

Read 1 Corinthians 13:8-13.

Love never ends. But as for prophecies, they will come to an end; as for tongues, they will cease; as for knowledge, it will come to an end. ⁹ For we know only in part, and we prophesy only in part; ¹⁰ but when the complete comes, the partial will come to an end. ¹¹ When I was a child, I spoke like a child, I thought like a child, I reasoned like a child; when I became an adult, I put an end to childish ways. ¹² For now we see in a mirror, dimly, but then we will see face to face. Now I know only in part; then I will know fully, even as I have been fully known. ¹³ And now faith, hope, and love abide, these three; and the greatest of these is love.

Paul made no bones about it: The Corinthians were acting like children. Verse 11 reiterates Paul's earlier reference to them as children in chapter 3 of the same letter. This letter would not have been fun to read (or to listen to as it was read aloud to the congregation, which was more likely).

> *In what ways do you think understanding your own gifts can be helpful to the community? In what ways can the community keep those gifts in the proper framework of love?*

Workers Ahead

Here was a congregation of people who seemed to think of themselves as spiritually advanced. They were so advanced that they understood the spiritual gifts and had deep theological discussions about them. Some people believed their particular gift proved a level of spiritual maturity beyond all others. Rebuking them, Paul called into question their thoughts, feelings, and understandings regarding spiritual gifts. "Stop acting like children," Paul told them. "You have completely missed the point."

It is so easy to get caught up in the present! We all know people who either cannot look beyond the present circumstances, or choose not to do so. The Corinthians were focusing too much on the present rather than the eternal future about which Paul had preached.

> *In what ways do you see the Corinthian's behavior exhibited today? Do you think the Christian Church has gone to the opposite extreme? Why or why not? Which behavior do you witness in your community? in your church?*

Paul, like Jesus, always seems to have used examples with which the people would have been familiar. In verse 12, he used an analogy about looking in a mirror. This analogy helped the peple to understand that they could see God's kingdom from where they were, but not as clearly as they would one day.

One of the well-known industries of the city of Corinth was mirror-making. Throughout Paul's writings, it is clear that he knew his audience. This is just another example of the ways in which he used the congregation's culture and geography to help them better understand his teachings.

As a class, create a responsive litany, a prayer, or a dramatic reading based on 1 Corinthians 13. Work together on ways you would like to see this chapter used in worship. When complete, share it with your pastor or worship team, and ask that it be used at an appropriate time during the year.

Suggest to your pastor or session that the church engage in a study on spiritual gifts. As people learn about the gifts and are helped to identify the ones they possess, they will be more likely to use them. Remind people that their gifts can change and new ones develop over time, so they should not assume that their gifts are the same as they once were

Reflect about which spiritual gifts you have. Think about the ones that other people seem to have. Take notes so that when you finally do a spiritual gifts inventory, you can see what was clear and what was surpising.

> What analogies could you use to help people understand God's love?

> If your congregation has engaged in a study on spiritual gifts, what was that experience like for the church? What did you learn about yourself? What surprises came out of the study?

In the Rear View

Paul had a lot to say about love, as did Jesus. They both told people to live in love, that love is above all else. Yet, the Corinthians got Paul's teachings all wrong.

We've all had the experience of hearing something one way, while the person right next to us heard something entirely different. I'm sure Paul taught them about love for God and for one another. Yet, their human natures kicked in, and they found themselves seeking to rise to the top, even at the expense of others.

Paul's letter would have been a bitter pill to swallow for people who thought they were spiritually superior, but it also offered hope to those whose gifts had been deemed less important. In a world where love rules, everyone is appreciated equally for the gifts he or she contributes to the community.

Travel Log

Day 1:
Find a quiet place where you won't be disturbed. Read 1 Corinthians 13 slowly. Breathe deeply and in rhythm as you simply sit in the presence of God. After five minutes of silence, write about the true nature of your love as an action. Reflect on what you have written. What surprises you about your true relationship with love?

Day 2:
According to Paul's writings, love is more action than emotion. Spend time thinking about this difference. In what ways do you agree? How do you disagree? Write your reflections below, or sketch or paint a picture comparing and contrasting love as action vs. love as emotion.

Day 3:

One of the significant things the Corinthians were doing wrong was comparing themselves to one another. Paul's letter pointed out the ways in which individuals thought more highly of themselves others. If some people felt superior, there were also those who were made to feel "less than." Face the ways you have been made to feel "less than." Write a few words or sentences about your feelings. Ask God to help you forgive those who have made you feel this way.

Day 4:

Yesterday you were invited to think about the ways in which you have been made to feel "less than." What may require even more bravery is reflecting on the ways in which you have made someone else feel "less than." Journal about specific instances when you created a false hierarchy that allowed you to feel justified in doing this. Confess the ways in which you have caused others to feel inferior. Know that God loves and forgives you.

Day 5:
Even if you haven't taken a spiritual gifts inventory, you may have an idea as to what one or more of your gifts is. Reflect on where you see God using you and how your gifts are part of your service to God. In what ways do you find love in those situations? How do the ways in which you are using your gifts fulfilling you? If you do not feel fulfilled, how can you change the ways you are using your gift?

Day 6:
Imagine God has called you to write a letter to your congregation about love, spiritual gifts, and living "the way" of Christ. Remember the ways in which Paul used the culture and geography of a place to connect with his readers. Your letter may be one of rebuke like Paul's, or it may be a one of praise. Begin writing to see what emerges rather than trying to compose the letter in your mind first. It may be helpful to set a timer for 10 minutes and begin with "Dear congregation, I am writing to let you know that I see you following Christ by…" Write until the timer sounds; don't stop to correct or be concerned about how you have worded something. Read what you have written, and reflect on what this tells you about your own relationship with your church.

Day 7:
Read 1 Corinthians 13 in a version of the Bible different than the one you usually use. Read it a second time, aloud. Breathe deeply and take in every word as you read the passage. Write down images, words, or phrases that jump out at you. Rest in the knowledge that God is love.

Sources:
"BibleGateway".com: *A Searchable Online Bible in over 100 Versions and 50 Languages. IVP NT Commentary Series.* N.p., n.d. Web.

Hays, Richard B. "Spiritual Manifestations in Worship (12:1-14:40)." *First Corinthians: A Bible Commentary for Teaching and Preaching.* Louisville: John Knox, 1997. 221-230. Print.

Love Is from God

Scripture for lesson:
1 John 4:7-21

Written by Tiffany Hall McClung

When I look back on my high school friendships in small town Alabama, I am shocked by the theological discussions that were a consistent part of our lunch times. Over our rectangular pieces of pizza and canned corn, we would debate the ways in which God works in the world. I was the only Presbyterian at the table; most of my friends were Baptist. My best friend, Stephanie, and I really enjoyed debating the religious issues of the day. Sometimes our discussions grew so heated that our other friends gradually became silent as they watched the two of us debate God, the afterlife, and why we believed what we did.

One day as I listened to Stephanie, I became very confused. Although I don't remember the exact conversation, I have a vague recollection of hell being mentioned at some point. Suddenly, a light pierced the fog of my confusion, and I replied to her, "Oooohhhhh. Now I get it. Everything you believe is grounded in fear, which I can't understand. All that I believe is grounded in love." I wasn't trying to sound "holier than thou," but I don't remember much conversation continuing that day. It was a formative moment for me. I may not remember all the details, but I don't think I'll ever forget the realization that some people's faith is grounded in fear. I count myself lucky to have had parents who grounded my own faith in love.

> How do you feel about faith being grounded in fear? in love? In what is your faith grounded?

Prep for the Journey

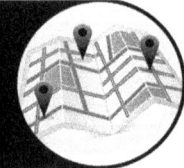

In the introduction to First John in *The Message*, Eugene Peterson wrote, "The two most difficult things to get straight in life are love and God. More often than not, the mess people make of their lives can be traced to failure or stupidity or meanness in one or both of these areas" (503). In what some consider to be more of a homily than a letter, First John is the author's attempt to correct this kind of mess.

Most scholars agree that First John was written by the Apostle believed to have written the Gospel of John. The two contain many similarities such as the use of the terms *light*, *life*, and *love*. First John was not sent to a specific church, but was likely shared by traveling missionaries when they visited the many house churches of that time.

Likely while in Ephesus around 85-95 C.E., John found the need to address some issues in the community that he loved. This homily addresses the origin of love, after John had watched those he referred to as "beloved" behaving poorly with one another.

Read 1 John 4:7-10.

Beloved, let us love one another, because love is from God; everyone who loves is born of God and knows God. ⁸ Whoever does not love does not know God, for God is love. ⁹ God's love was revealed among us in this way: God sent his only Son into the world so that we might live through him. ¹⁰ In this is love, not that we loved God but that he loved us and sent his Son to be the atoning sacrifice for our sins.

Although First John was not addressed to a specific group, the use of personal pronouns indicates a personal relationship with the intended hearers. We know John wrote it for the benefit of Christians communities in response to false teachings that were pervading the community. This writing reflects an extreme diversity of faith, which was of great concern to the author. Wanting to make sure that the people were clear about the one, true God, John taught about love—where it comes from and what one should do with it.

From the beginning of our scripture passage, John made his topic clear: "You must love one another." John didn't simply state the need for love; he provided information on its origin.

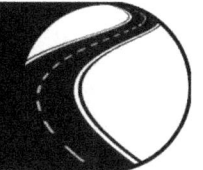

Defining love can be next to impossible, but John's words help us to recognize love. We often say, "God is love," but John added, "God gives us love." Because God loves us so much, God has given us the gift that is love. Jesus, the Christ, is the physical and spiritual evidence of God's gift of love. We respond to that gift by loving others. In turn, the love we show to others is the physical and spiritual evidence of God's love to the world. Only through this love can we truly know God. Without this love, there would be no evidence of God's love in the world.

Read 1 John 4:11-17.

Beloved, since God loved us so much, we also ought to love one

---

If we think of love as action, how do the relationships between members of your congregation show evidence of God's love to the world? In what ways are you lacking in this evidence? Talk about ways to increase evidence of God's love through the relationships within your own congregation.

How would you distinguish between "God is love" and "God gives us love"?

another. ¹² *No one has ever seen God; if we love one another, God lives in us, and his love is perfected in us.*

¹³ *By this we know that we abide in him and he in us, because he has given us of his Spirit.* ¹⁴ *And we have seen and do testify that the Father has sent his Son as the Savior of the world.* ¹⁵ *God abides in those who confess that Jesus is the Son of God, and they abide in God.* ¹⁶ *So we have known and believe the love that God has for us.*

*God is love, and those who abide in love abide in God, and God abides in them.*¹⁷ *Love has been perfected among us in this: that we may have boldness on the day of judgment, because as he is, so are we in this world.*

Some scholars believe this passage to be one of the most beautifully written and eloquent statements about love in the New Testament. John's use of poetic language certainly places it in the running! Even in the midst of such flowery language, the message is clear: We can't see God. We can't really know God aside from the love we have for one another. Therefore, if we want to share the love of God with the world, we must show love for one another.

In a world that values the image so much that a meme can attract more attention than a newscast, priority is placed on what is visible and seen. This is nothing new, really. We focus on what we can see. (Even saying "focus" is a reference to how our eyes work to see images.) John found groups of believers in turmoil as they argued over what was seen and what was not seen. Some people in those communities had begun to say that the unseen Christ could never have been a physical being who lived as Jesus of Nazareth. Their assertions led to arguments and discord. While John addressed the specific problem elsewhere, he challenged the people to focus on what they could see while believing in what they couldn't. "No one can see God. But, people do see how 'the people of God' treat one another." Again, if we want the world to know God's love, we are the ones who have to show it.

In addition, John reaffirmed the gift that God has given us. We may not have seen God with our own eyes, but God loves us so much that God sent Christ into the world. God lives in those who confess Christ. Not only does God live in them, but God makes Christ's love perfect in them.

As I read First John, I can almost hear the pleading nature of his voice, begging those reading or hearing his words to see how simple it really is. But we want to see for ourselves. We want to touch Jesus, to talk with him so that we know we are loved. We want to see Jesus to know that it is safe to love others. Loving blindly is scary. It makes us afraid. So afraid, in fact, that we often find ourselves holding back, withholding our love from others, which means that we don't experience as much of God's love. When we withhold our love, not only do we suffer, but John said the whole world would suffer. Without Christians continuing to share the gift of love God has given us, the world will not know God.

Meme: a cultural item in the form of an image, video, phrase, etc., that is spread via the Internet and often altered in a creative or humorous way (Dictionary.com, October 19, 2015).

When have you been challenged to believe in what you couldn't see? How do you show God's love to the world?

Imagine a world that does not need the love between people as evidence of God's love. What would that world look like? How would its inhabitants know God and God's love? What other evidence of God's love do you see in your life?

Scenic Route

Read 1 John 4:-18-21.

There is no fear in love, but perfect love casts out fear; for fear has to do with punishment, and whoever fears has not reached perfection in love. 19 We love because he first loved us. 20 Those who say, "I love God," and hate their brothers or sisters, are liars; for those who do not love a brother or sister whom they have seen, cannot love God whom they have not seen. 21 The commandment we have from him is this: those who love God must love their brothers and sisters also.

John may have been quite the poet, but in these verses he didn't hold back. To paraphrase John, "If you say you love God, but you hate others, you are a liar." For John, the two things could not and would not coexist.

In addition to living in a world that places more value on the image than the word, it also feeds on the fears of others. Unfortunately, some people in the American Christian Church have adopted this worldly view as well. When we teach our youth through fear-based doctrine, we are doing just the opposite of what John told people was the very essence of God—love. Too often the idea of the punishment of hell is what motivates people in their faith and relationship with God. For John, this idea simply would not do. Love must conquer fear—even fear that seems to motivate right living—because fear will not ultimately show God's love to the world. Instead, fear will hide God's love. "There is no fear in love…"

John wrote this letter in an effort to correct a terrible problem, one that history tells us was heresy. Rather than writing a letter filled with threats of punishment and talk of eternal damnation, John referred again and again to the hearers as "beloved" and spoke poetically of the love of God being shared between neighbors. It is clear that John believed the answer to the problem (and all problems) was love. While we may argue among ourselves about what that love can look like, John pointed to Christ as evidence of God's gift of love. Christ is the image of love we are to model in the world. The responsibility is great. We must love others and show that love in the way that Christ intends, or God's love will not be visible.

How do you feel when someone is very direct in "telling it like it is"? How do you react when the message applies to you?

What motivates you in your faith relationship? How do you feel about using fear to motivate a person toward right living?

How does the way someone approaches you affect the way you receive the message he or she brings? How might you need to modify the way you approach people so that they will be more receptive to God's message?

In what ways can you participate in a culture that feeds and breeds fear without doing so yourself? Identify one way you have fed the fears within yourself and others. Strategize ways to end that behavior.

Workers Ahead

Loving as Christ loved can be very scary. It means leaving your comfort zone to minister to and with people whom you think are very different from you or who speak a different language. It may mean putting your life in jeopardy by going to war-torn countries or caring for people who are sick and/or dying. It may mean taking a stand against unfair policies, even when you or your friends and family benefit from them.

Spend time in small groups sharing your fears about sharing God's love. Do you feel fear where other nationalities are concerned? What about other age groups? Or those who interpret scripture differently? Find the willingness to be honest about the ways these fears keep you from loving others. You may be surprised to learn that others have some of the same fears. Remember that the scripture tells us fear and love can't coexist.

Now that you have admitted your fears, consider ways of facing and, eventually, overcoming them. Some possibilities might be to volunteer at a homeless shelter, learn a different language, or become acquainted with people who have different beliefs. After all, we are all God's children.

Imagine as a class how you can better show love to your community. Be specific and concrete. Make a list that includes steps for achieving the shared ideas. Find ways to make them happen. Consider involving the rest of your faith community in the efforts.

In the Rear View

How are you willing to get your hands dirty to show God's love? How can you encourage others to do so as well?

John's entire message focused on love—God's love for us and how we share that love with others. This type of love is not shallow with sentimentality, but involves getting your hands dirty, taking action. In a society that is becoming increasingly less personal, taking action may seem revolutionary. We would often much rather give money for something than to become personally involved. Giving money to a project is not a bad thing, but we should each find a way we can share God's love. How else will we truly know God?

Travel Log

Day 1:

Find a quiet place where you will not be disturbed. Read 1 John 4:7-21 slowly. Sit silently while you listen for God to reveal your fears about showing love. Breathe deeply and in rhythm as you simply sit in the presence of God. Then reflect on and write about your experience for approximately 5 minutes. What things did God reveal that surprised you? How are you going to address those issues?

Day 2:

Eugene Peterson wrote, "The two most difficult things to get straight in life are love and God. More often than not, the mess people make of their lives can be traced to failure or stupidity or meanness in one or both of these areas." Reflecting on this quote. You may want to write it on a card and carry it with you. Make some notes in the space below in regards to how you agree or disagree with Peterson.

Day 3:

Find magazines that you are willing to tear up. Collect paper, magazines, markers, pens, pencils, and glue. Spend a few minutes defining "love" and thinking about John's assertion that the way we see God is by seeing the love between God's children. Spend some time quietly reflecting on this idea. When you are ready, use the materials you have (magazines, markers, etc.) to make a collage or picture that represents your ideas on this subject.

Day 4:

Identify a conflict in your own life. Journal about this conflict, reflecting on the ways that fear plays a role in maintaining the conflict. Use your imagination to help you devise a creative solution to the conflict—a solution based in love. Note the conflict and the solution below.

Day 5:

Gather crayons, markers, and/or colored pencils. Set a timer for 10 minutes. Before starting the timer, read these instructions: 1. Write the word *fear* just below these instructions. 2. Write the word *punishment* slightly above the instructions for Day 6. As you begin the timer, reflect on the ways in which fear has been used to punish you. Also reflect on the ways you have punished others by using fear. Then simply doodle. Using the colors, make lines or shapes as you pray about fear and punishment. When the 10 minutes has ended, look at your creation.

Day 6:

Today turn your attention toward Jesus. Look up a story in the Gospels that you believe best represents Christ showing love to others. (Use a passage other than the Crucifixion.) Journal about the actions Jesus modeled and how you can follow his example in your own life.

Day 7:

Read 1 John 4:7-21 again. Now read it a second time more slowly. Breathe deeply, and take in every word as you read the passage. Write down images, words, or phrases that jump out at you. Remember that God loves you deeply—no matter what.

Sources:

"BibleGateway."com: *A Searchable Online Bible in over 100 Versions and 50 Languages. IVP NT Commentary Series.* N.p., n.d. Web.

Meeks, Wayne A. ed. *The Harper Collins Study Bible: New Revised Standard Version.* London: HarperCollins Publishers, 1989. Print.

Peterson, Eugene. *The Message: The New Testament, Psalms, and Proverbs.* Colorado Springs: NavPress, 1995. 503. Print.

Smith, D. Moody. "1 John 4:7-12" *First, Second, and Third John: Interpretation: A Bible Commentary for Teaching and Preaching.* Louisville: John Knox, 1991. 106-111. Print.

www.ingramcontent.com/pod-product-compliance
Lightning Source LLC
Chambersburg PA
CBHW081501040426
42446CB00016B/3339